4

Zaner-Bloser

Handwriting

Author

Clinton S. Hackney, Ed.D.

Reviewers

Credits

Art: Josh Hara: 5; John Hovell: 3, 4, 15, 16, 17, 20, 21, 22, 25, 27, 30, 31, 41, 60, 79, 84, 86, 87, 94; Tom Leonard: 33, 53, 54, 57, 73, 80, 84, 90, 94; Jane McCreary: 63, 68, 74, 82; Sharron O'Neil: 3, 4, 35, 37, 39, 46, 49, 51, 88, 89; Shel Silverstein: 6, 92

Photos: George C. Anderson Photography, Inc.: 5, 10, 11; Stephen Ogilvy: 12, 13, 14, 18, 44

Literature: "It's Dark in Here" from *Where the Sidewalk Ends* by Shel Silverstein. Copyright © 1974 by Evil Eye Music, Inc.

Development: Kirchoff/Wohlberg, Inc., in collaboration with Zaner-Bloser Educational Publishers

ISBN 0-7367-1214-3

04 05 06 159 5 4

Zaner-Bloser, Inc., P.O. Box 16764, Columbus, Ohio 43216-6764
1-800-421-3018
www.zaner-bloser.com
Printed in the United States of America

Contents

Unit 1: Getting Started

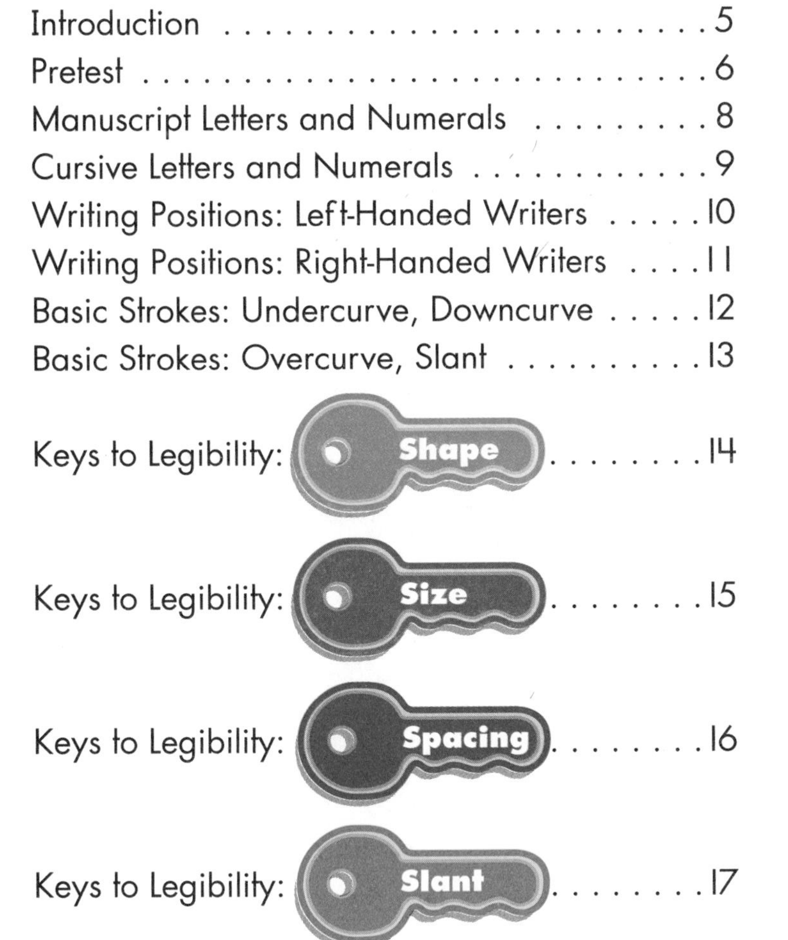

Unit 2: Writing Lowercase Letters

Unit 3: Writing Uppercase Letters

Unit 4: Writing for Yourself

Unit 5: Writing for Someone Else

Unit 6: Writing for Publication

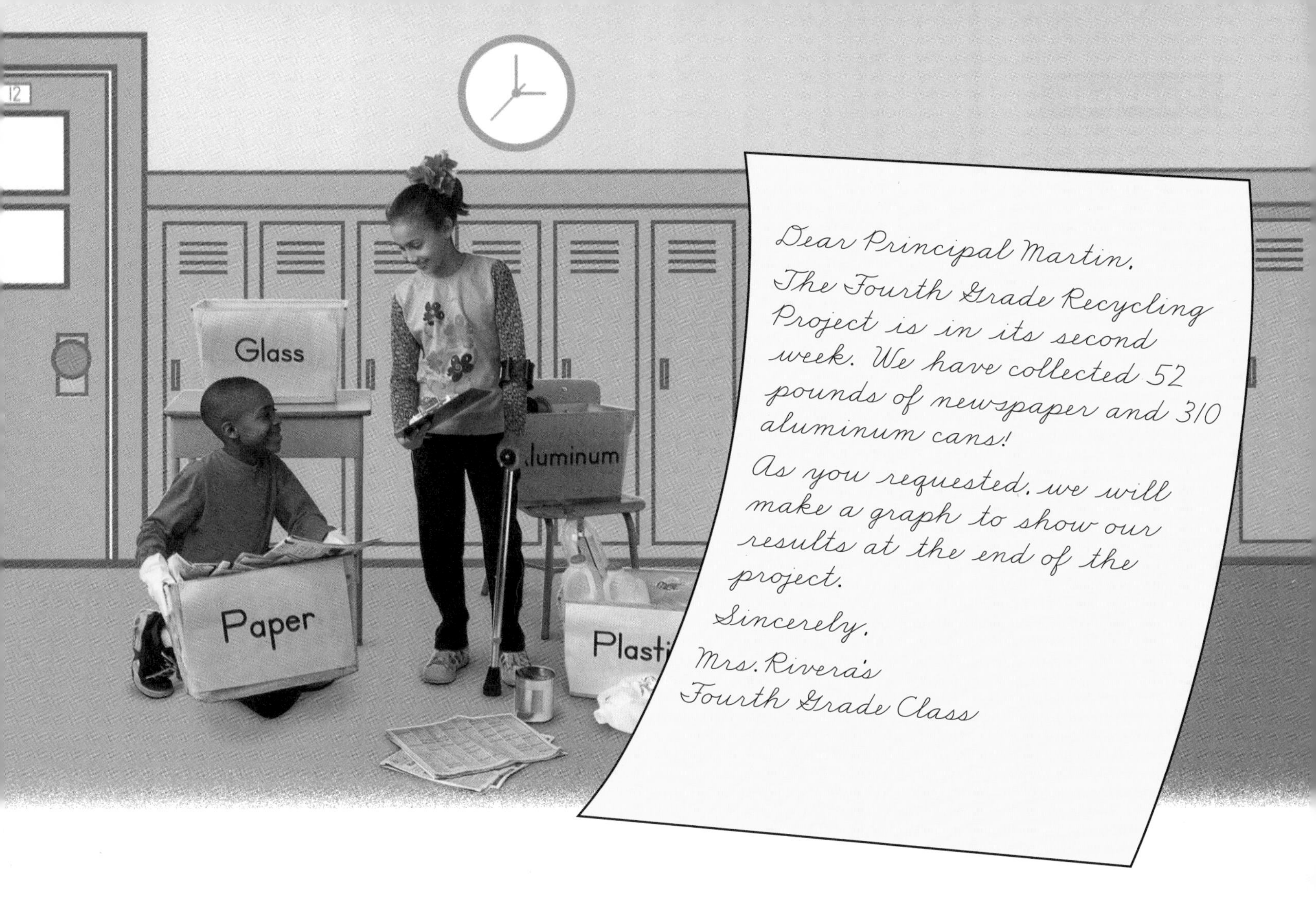

Dear Principal Martin,

The Fourth Grade Recycling Project is in its second week. We have collected 52 pounds of newspaper and 310 aluminum cans!

As you requested, we will make a graph to show our results at the end of the project.

Sincerely,

Mrs. Rivera's
Fourth Grade Class

You write for many reasons at school, at home, and in your community. The lessons in this book will help you write legibly so you and other people can easily read what you have written.

Evaluating your own handwriting is a good habit to form. When you see the **Stop and Check** sign in this book, stop and circle the best letter you wrote on that line.

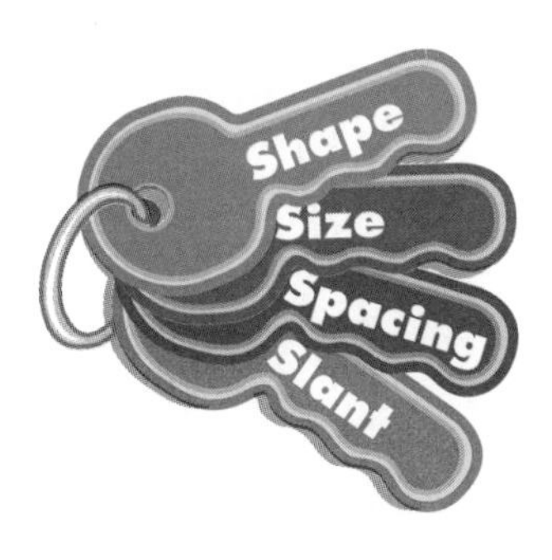

You will see the **Keys to Legibility** throughout this book. They will help you remember to check the **shape, size, spacing,** and **slant** of your writing to make sure it is easy to read.

Pretest

It's Dark in Here

I am writing these poems
From inside a lion,
And it's rather dark in here.
So please excuse the handwriting
Which may not be too clear.
But this afternoon by the lion's cage
I'm afraid I got too near.
And I'm writing these lines
From inside a lion,
And it's rather dark in here.

by Shel Silverstein

Write the poem in your best cursive handwriting.

Is your writing easy to read? Yes No

Write your five best cursive letters.

Write five cursive letters you would like to improve.

Manuscript Letters and Numerals

Aa Bb Cc Dd Ee Ff Gg
Hh Ii Jj Kk Ll Mm Nn
Oo Pp Qq Rr Ss Tt Uu
Vv Ww Xx Yy Zz

1 2 3 4 5 6 7 8 9 10

Although most of your writing will be in cursive, you will still use manuscript for such things as address books, labeling, and signs. Use your best manuscript to write the following.

1. Write your name.

2. Write a friend's name.

3. Write your initials and a friend's initials.

4. Write your ZIP code and state abbreviation.

Use one of the following ideas. Use manuscript to write a sign for your classroom door.

Come In | Please Knock | Welcome | Testing

Cursive Letters and Numerals

Aa Bb Cc Dd Ee Ff Gg

Hh Ii Jj Kk Ll Mm

Nn Oo Pp Qq Rr Ss Tt

Uu Vv Ww Xx Yy Zz

1 2 3 4 5 6 7 8 9 10

Use your best cursive to write the following.

1. Write your name.

2. Write the name of your school.

3. Write the numerals from 1 to 10.

4. Write the lowercase letters you think you use most.

5. Write the letters and numerals you want to improve.

Writing Positions

Left-Handed Writers

Sit like this.
Sit comfortably.
Lean forward a little.
Keep your feet flat on the floor.

Place the paper like this.

Slant the paper as shown in the picture.

Rest both arms on the desk. Use your right hand to shift the paper as you write.

Pull the pencil toward your left elbow when you write.

Hold the pencil like this.

Hold the pencil with your thumb and first two fingers.

Keep your first finger on top.

Bend your thumb and keep it on the side.

Do not squeeze the pencil when you write.

Right-Handed Writers

Sit like this.
Sit comfortably.
Lean forward a little.
Keep your feet flat on the floor.

Place the paper like this.

Slant the paper as shown in the picture.

Rest both arms on the desk. Use your left hand to shift the paper as you write.

Pull the pencil toward the middle of your body when you write.

Hold the pencil like this.

Hold the pencil with your thumb and first two fingers.

Keep your first finger on top.

Bend your thumb and keep it on the side.

Do not squeeze the pencil when you write.

Basic Strokes

Undercurve

An **undercurve** is one of the basic strokes used to write cursive letters. An undercurve stroke swings up.

Find an undercurve stroke at the beginning of each letter. Write the letters.

b e h j p t w

B G L P R S

Downcurve

A **downcurve** is one of the basic strokes used to write cursive letters. A downcurve stroke dives down.

Find a downcurve stroke at the beginning of each letter. Write the letters.

a c d g o q

A C D E O

Overcurve

An **overcurve** is one of the basic strokes used to write cursive letters. An overcurve stroke bounces up.

Find an overcurve stroke at the beginning of each letter. Write the letters.

m n v x y z

I J Q

Slant

A **slant** is one of the basic strokes used to write cursive letters. A slant stroke slides.

Find a slant stroke in each letter. Write the letters.

a d g i j m y

A B K R U X Y

Keys to Legibility

Make your writing easy to read. As you write cursive, pay attention to the shape of your writing.

There are four basic strokes in cursive writing.
Be sure to write each letter with good basic strokes.

undercurve

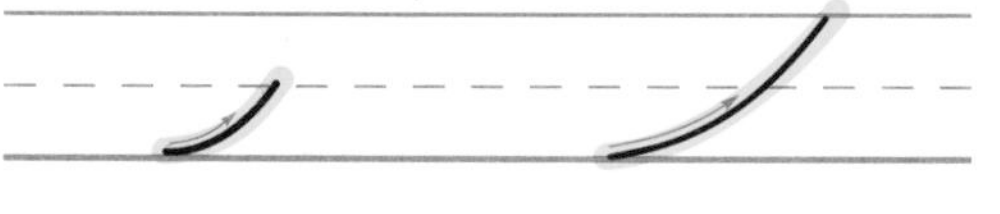

Write letters with undercurve strokes.

downcurve

Write letters with downcurve strokes.

a d C O

overcurve

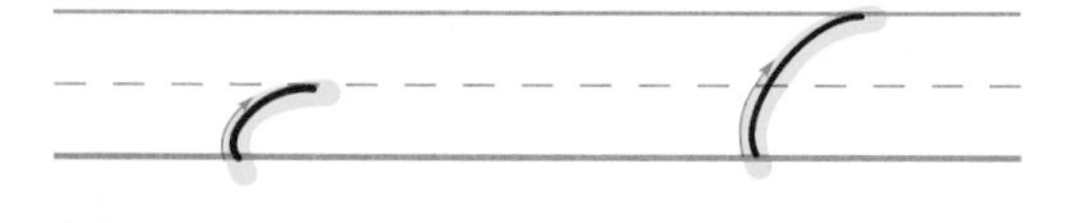

Write letters with overcurve strokes.

slant

Write letters with slant strokes.

t p B R

Make your writing easy to read. As you write cursive, pay attention to the size of your writing.

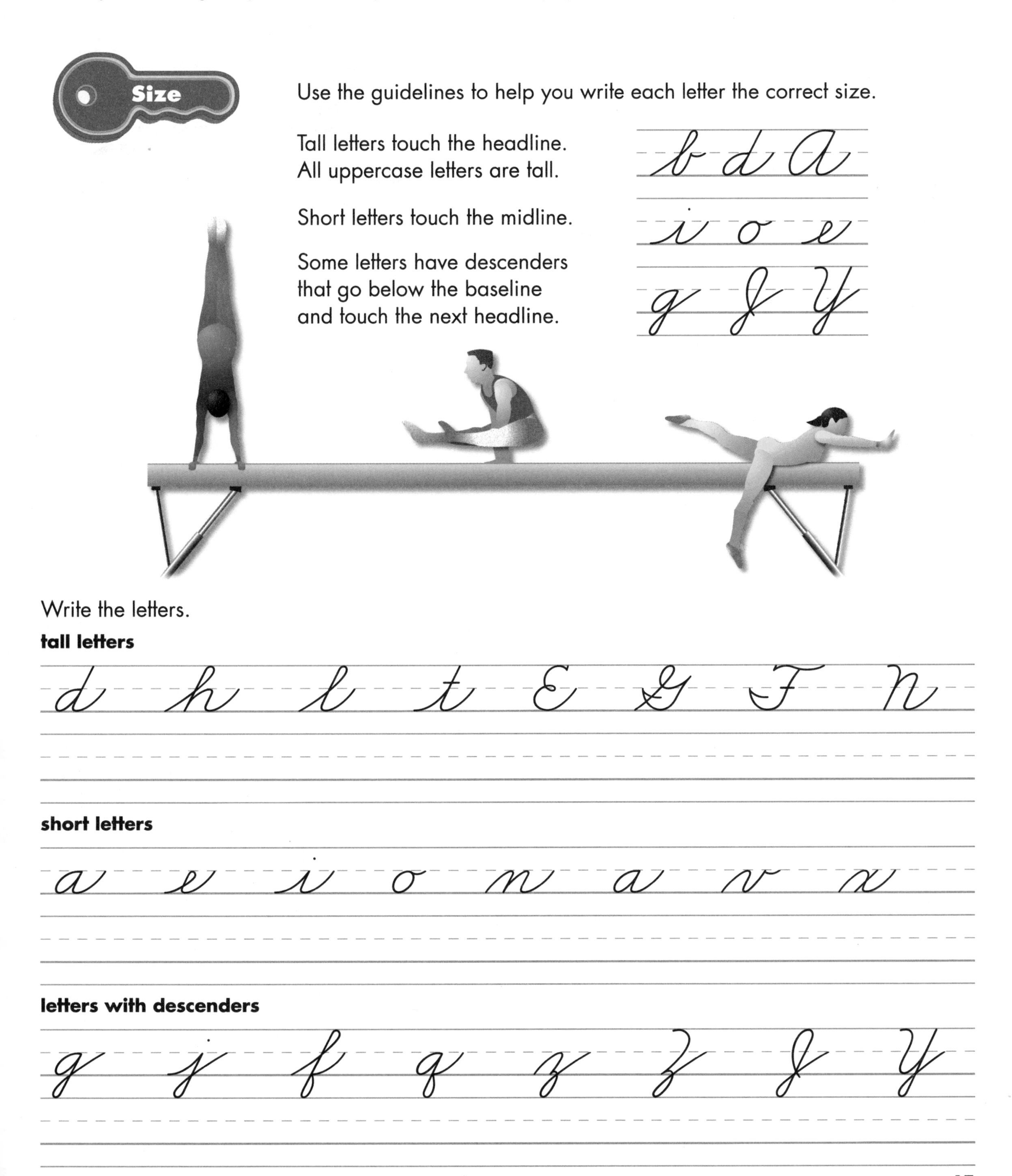

Use the guidelines to help you write each letter the correct size.

Tall letters touch the headline.
All uppercase letters are tall.

Short letters touch the midline.

Some letters have descenders that go below the baseline and touch the next headline.

Write the letters.

tall letters

short letters

letters with descenders

Keys to Legibility

Make your writing easy to read. As you write cursive, pay attention to the spacing of your writing.

Between Letters There should be enough space for O.

handwriting

Between Words There should be enough space for \.

between words

Between Sentences There should be enough space for O.

Spacing is important. So are shape and size.

Write the sentences. Use correct spacing between letters, words, and sentences.

My writing is neat. It has good spacing.

Make your writing easy to read. As you write cursive, pay attention to the slant of your writing.

Cursive letters have a uniform forward slant.

forward slant

To write with good slant:

POSITION • Check your paper position.

PULL • Pull your downstrokes in the proper direction.

SHIFT • Shift your paper as you write.

If you are left-handed . . .

Shift your paper as you write. Pull downstrokes to your left elbow.

If you are right-handed . . .

Shift your paper as you write. Pull downstrokes to the middle of your body.

Write the sentence. Check to see if your slant is uniform.

This is good slant.

Writing Lowercase Letters

To write legibly in cursive, you must form and join lowercase letters correctly. The lessons in this unit will show you how.

As you write, you will focus on shape, size, spacing, and slant to help make your writing legible.

a b c d e f
g h i j k l
m n o p q r
s t u v w x
y z

Write the lowercase cursive alphabet.

Circle your three best letters. Underline three letters you want to improve.

Beginning Strokes

The lowercase letters are grouped by their beginning strokes.

Undercurve Letters

Trace undercurve strokes.

Trace letters that begin with an undercurve.

i t u w e l b
h f k r s j p

Downcurve Letters

Trace downcurve strokes.

Trace letters that begin with a downcurve.

a d g o c q

Overcurve Letters

Trace overcurve strokes.

Trace letters that begin with an overcurve.

n m y x v z

Joinings

Before you join one letter to another, look at the way the letter ends.

Some letters end with undercurves. *i e t l s*

Some letters end with checkstrokes. *w v o b*

Some letters end with overcurves. *j y g z*

The letter *i* ends with an undercurve. Look at the ways *i* may be joined to other letters.

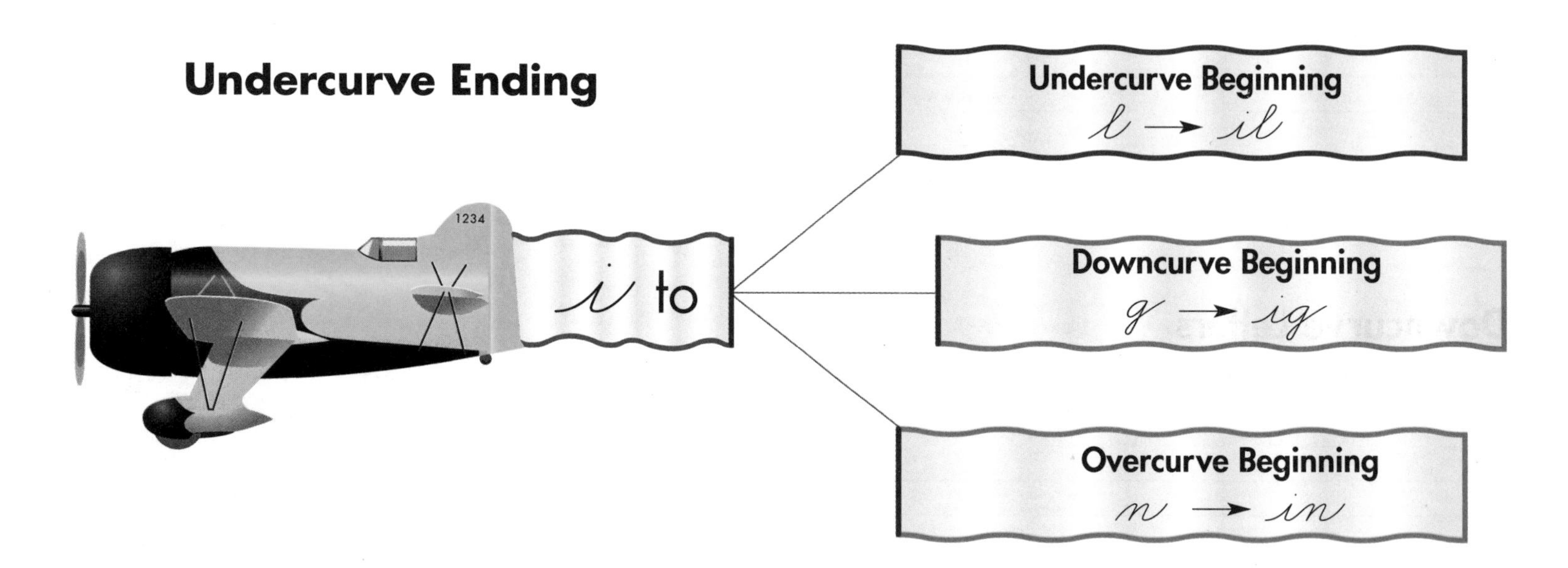

Write the joinings.

Undercurve to Undercurve	Undercurve to Downcurve	Undercurve to Overcurve
le pr	ea no	ry az
st fl	ag ic	sn ty

The letter *g* ends with an overcurve. Look at the ways *g* may be joined to other letters.

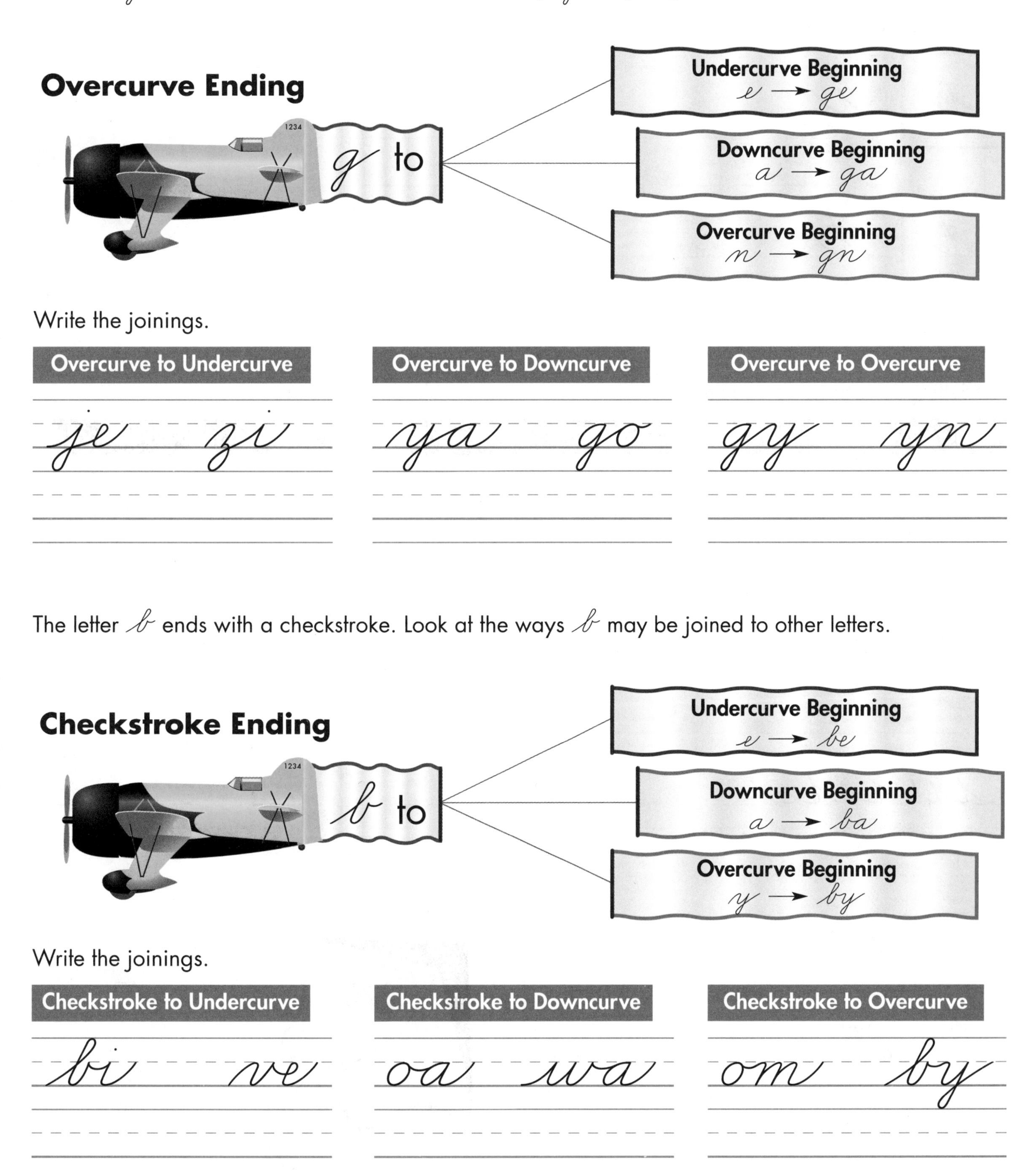

The letter *b* ends with a checkstroke. Look at the ways *b* may be joined to other letters.

Write the joinings.

Checkstroke to Undercurve

bi ve

Checkstroke to Downcurve

oa wa

Checkstroke to Overcurve

om by

Write Undercurve Letters

An undercurve ⁄ begins each letter. Write the letters.

i *i* *i* *i* *i* *i* *i*

t *t* *t* *t* *t* *t* *t*

The letters *i* and *t* end with an undercurve. Write the joinings and words.

Undercurve to Undercurve	Undercurve to Downcurve	Undercurve to Overcurve
it *tw*	*id* *ta*	*in* *ty*
kite	*glide*	*wind*
twists	*tail*	*gusty*

Better *Letters*

Be careful not to loop back. Write:

i not *i* *t* not *t*

Use your best handwriting to write the letters again.

An undercurve begins each letter. Write the letters.

u u

w w

The letter u ends with an undercurve. The letter w ends with a checkstroke.

Write the joinings and words.

Undercurve to Downcurve

ua ug

square

huge

Undercurve to Overcurve

um un

volume

pound

Checkstroke to Undercurve

we wi

weight

width

Better Letters

Be careful not to loop back. Write:

u not e w not e

Use your best handwriting to write the letters again.

Shape

Circle three letters you wrote that have good shape.

Write Undercurve Letters

An undercurve begins each letter. Write the letters.

e e

l l

The letters e and l end with an undercurve. Write the joinings and words.

Undercurve to Undercurve	Undercurve to Downcurve	Undercurve to Overcurve
er ls	ea lo	en ly
writer	read	send
e-mails	log on	quickly

Better *Letters*

Keep your loops open. Write:

e not e l not l

Use your best handwriting to write the letters again.

Shape

Circle your three best letters that have an undercurve ending.

Practice

Write the words and phrases.

inventions

screen start link

computer web sites

bulletin board laptop

printer disk on-line

CHECKSTROKE ALERT Join *w* and *r* at the midline. Write the joinings and words.

wr wr wr write

wrist wrap

Shape

Keys to Legibility

My writing has good shape. ☐

Write Undercurve Letters

An undercurve begins each letter. Write the letters.

b b b b b b b

h h h h h h h

The letter b ends with a checkstroke. The letter h ends with an undercurve.
Write the joinings and words.

Checkstroke to Undercurve	Checkstroke to Downcurve	Undercurve to Undercurve
bi br	ba bo	he hu
bike	bars	helmet
brakes	boxcar	hum

Better *Letters*

Keep your loops open. Write:
b not b h not h

Use your best handwriting to write the letters again.

Size

Circle your three best tall letters.

An undercurve begins each letter. Write the letters.

f f f f f f f

k k k k k k k

The letters f and k end with an undercurve. Write the joinings and words.

Undercurve to Undercurve	Undercurve to Downcurve	Undercurve to Overcurve
fl ks	fo ka	fy ky
flow	foam	leafy
creeks	kayak	risky

Better *Letters*

Keep your loops open. Write:
f not f k not k

Use your best handwriting to write the letters again.

Write Undercurve Letters

An undercurve ⁄ begins each letter. Write the letters.

r r

s s

The letters r and s end with an undercurve. Write the joinings and words.

Undercurve to Undercurve	Undercurve to Downcurve	Undercurve to Overcurve
re su	rg so	rn sy
renew	energy	return
sun	solar	system

Better *Letters*

Be careful not to round r and s.
Write: r not r s not s

Use your best handwriting to write the letters again.

Size

Circle your three best short letters.

An undercurve begins each letter. Write the letters.

j j j j j j j

p p p p p p p

The letter j ends with an overcurve. The letter p ends with an undercurve.
Write the joinings and words.

Overcurve to Undercurve

ju je

jury

jest

Undercurve to Undercurve

pl pr

explain

process

Undercurve to Downcurve

po pa

point

pardon

Better *Letters*

Make sure to loop back. Write:
j not j p not p

Use your best handwriting to write the letters again.

Size

Circle your three best letters that have a descender.

Practice

Write the words.

sail ship

chart plot a course

explore rudder keel

forward aft deck

map jib starboard

JOINING ALERT

The undercurve to downcurve joining becomes a doublecurve.
Write the joinings and words.

pa sa fa package

sash fast

Shape
Size

Keys to Legibility

My writing has good shape. ☐
My writing has good size. ☐

Manuscript Maintenance

Play a word game of animal, vegetable, or mineral. Write **animal**, **vegetable**, or **mineral** in the box at the center of the web below. Then, choose five words from the list that fit your subject. Write them in the web in your best manuscript.

Write Downcurve Letters

A downcurve begins each letter. Write the letters.

a a a a a a a

d d d d d d d

The letters a and d end with an undercurve. Write the joinings and words.

Undercurve to Undercurve	Undercurve to Downcurve	Undercurve to Overcurve
ab di	ac dd	an dy
abacus	facts	change
divide	add	study

Better *Letters*

Close a and d. Write:
a not u d not d

Use your best handwriting to write the letters again.

Spacing

Circle a word you wrote that has good joinings.

A downcurve begins each letter. Write the letters.

g g

o o

The letter g ends with an overcurve. The letter o ends with a checkstroke.
Write the joinings and words.

Overcurve to Undercurve	Checkstroke to Undercurve	Checkstroke to Overcurve
gr ge	ob ol	on oy
green	global	one
oxygen	ecology	enjoy

Better *Letters*

Be careful to close g and o.
Write: g not g o not o

Use your best handwriting to write the letters again.

Write Downcurve Letters

A downcurve begins each letter. Write the letters.

c c c c c c c

q q q q q q q

The letters c and q end with an undercurve. Write the joinings and words.

Undercurve to Undercurve	Undercurve to Downcurve	Undercurve to Overcurve
qu qu	ca co	cy cn
quick	cartoon	bouncy
quip	comical	picnic

Better *Letters*

Be careful to close q. Write: q not q

Use your best handwriting to write the letters again.

Spacing

Circle a word you wrote that has good joinings.

Practice

Write the words and phrases.

rain forest

forest floor canopies

macaws salamanders

quiet humid rain

towering snakes

CHECKSTROKE ALERT Join *o* with other letters at the midline.

os or oo ecosystem

orchid bloom

Keys to Legibility

My writing has good shape. ☐
My writing has good size. ☐
My writing has good spacing. ☐

Write Overcurve Letters

An overcurve begins each letter. Write the letters.

n n

m m

The letters n and m end with an undercurve. Write the joinings and words.

Undercurve to Undercurve	Undercurve to Downcurve	Undercurve to Overcurve
nu me	nc ma	ny mn
number	zinc	shiny
metal	magnet	column

Better *Letters*

Be careful to round n and m.
Write: n not n m not m

Use your best handwriting to write the letters again.

Slant

Circle three letters you wrote that have good slant.

An overcurve begins each letter. Write the letters.

y y

x x

The letter y ends with an overcurve. The letter x ends with an undercurve.
Write the joinings and words.

Overcurve to Undercurve	Overcurve to Overcurve	Undercurve to Undercurve
ye ys	yn ym	xp xt
year	lynx	expect
days	symbol	next

Better *Letters*

Be careful to round y and x.
Write: y not y x not x

Use your best handwriting to write the letters again.

NOVEMBER

24 SUN	25 MON	26 TUE	27 WED	28 THUR	29 FRI	30 SAT
visit Grand-ma	Mom's birth-day	clean fish tank	last day of school this week	Thanks-giving	rake leaves	foot-ball game 4:00

Write Overcurve Letters

An overcurve begins each letter. Write the letters.

v v v v v v v

z z z z z z z

The letter v ends with a checkstroke. The letter z ends with an overcurve.
Write the joinings and words.

Checkstroke to Downcurve	Overcurve to Undercurve	Overcurve to Downcurve
va vo	ze zi	za zo
lava	haze	hazard
volcano	zigzag	zoom

Better *Letters*

Be careful to round v and z.
Write: v not v z not z

Use your best handwriting to write the letters again.

Slant

Circle two words you wrote that have good slant.

Practice

Write the words.

animals

ox viper fox

chimpanzee buzzard

yak hyena turkey

zebra zoo vulture

CHECKSTROKE ALERT Each word has a checkstroke joining at the midline. Write the words.

mouse ostrich boar

lion oxen

Keys to Legibility

Shape Size Spacing Slant

My writing has good shape. ☐
My writing has good size. ☐
My writing has good spacing. ☐
My writing has good slant. ☐

Lowercase Review

Write undercurve letters.

i t u w e l b

h f k r s j p

Write downcurve letters.

a d g o c q

Write overcurve letters.

n m y x v z

Circle your best letter in each group above. Write the letters you want to improve.

Write the joinings.

it ea ry ye ga wr bo

Manuscript Maintenance

Bicycle Parts

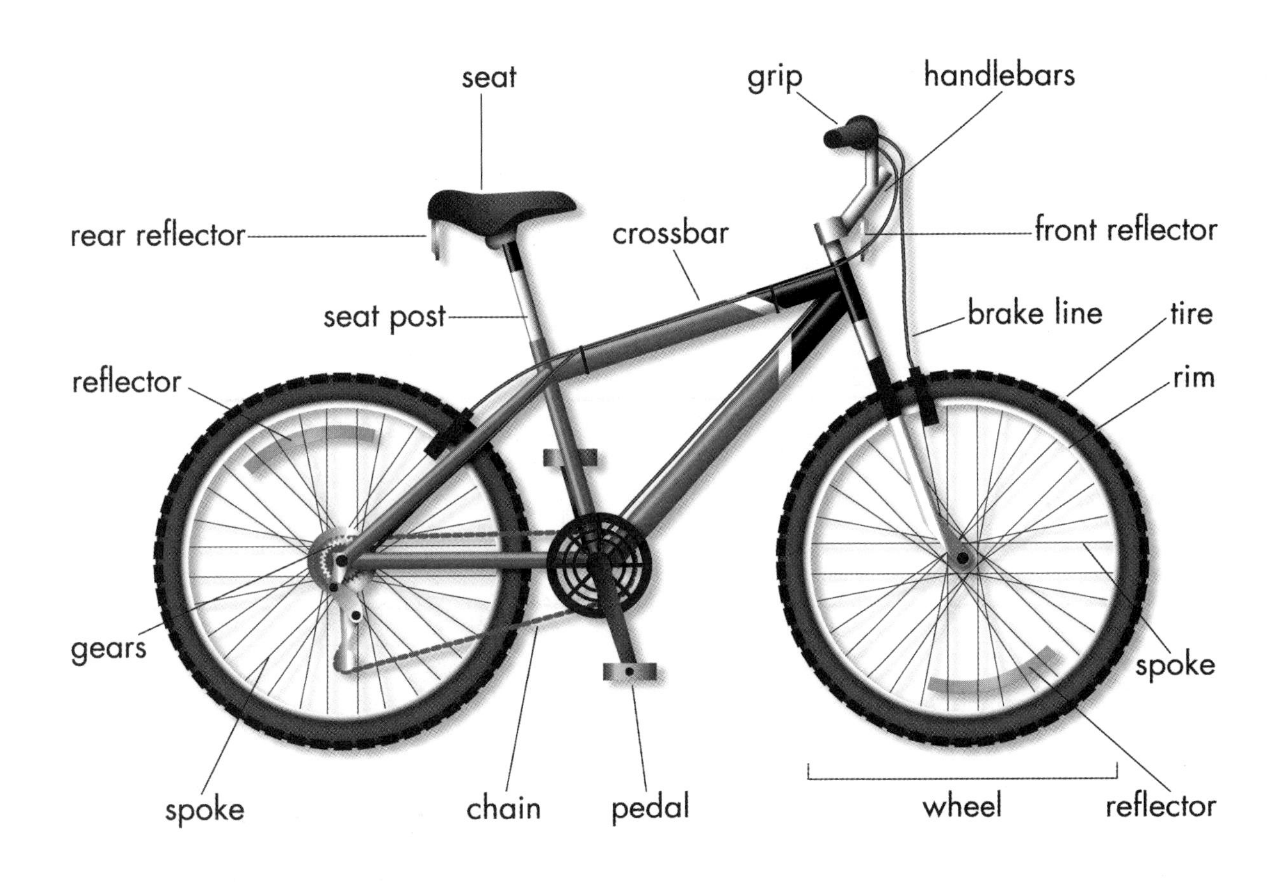

Unscramble the name of each bicycle part. Write the names in manuscript.

badlehanrs	atse
irpg	atse sopt
ehewl	ossrcarb
riet	deapl
mir	toreclfer
skope	ihcna

Cursive Numerals

Write the missing numerals.

14, 16, 18, ____, ____, 24, ____

Write the missing numerals.

78, 79, ____, ____, 82, 83, ____

Write the odd numbers between 1 and 13.

1, ____, ____, ____, ____, ____, 13

Write the even numbers between 10 and 20.

10, ____, ____, ____, ____, 20

Here are two magic squares. The sum of the numbers in a magic square's rows and columns is always the same. Fill in the missing numerals.

1		14	4
12	6	7	
	10	11	
13		2	16

Write these facts about time in your best cursive handwriting.

A minute is 60 seconds.

An hour is 60 minutes.

A day is 24 hours.

A week is 7 days.

A year is 12 months.

A year is 365 days.

A leap year is 366 days.

A decade is 10 years.

Writing Uppercase Letters

To write legibly in cursive, you must write uppercase letters well. In the lessons in this unit, the uppercase letters are grouped by common strokes. You will learn when to join an uppercase letter to the letter that follows.

As you write, you will focus on shape, size, spacing, and slant to help make your writing legible.

A B C D E F
G H I J K L
M N O P Q R
S T U V W X
Y Z

Write the uppercase cursive alphabet.

Circle your three best letters. Underline three letters you want to improve.

Beginning Strokes

The uppercase letters are grouped by their strokes.

Downcurve Letters

Trace downcurve strokes and letters.

A O D C E

Curve Forward Letters

Trace curve forward-slant strokes and curve forward letters.

N M H K

U Y V W X

Overcurve and Doublecurve Letters

Trace overcurve strokes and letters.

I J Q

Trace doublecurve strokes and letters.

T F

Undercurve-Loop and Undercurve-Slant Letters

Trace undercurve-loop strokes and letters.

G S L

Trace undercurve-slant strokes and letters.

P R B

Write Downcurve Letters

Find a downcurve (in each letter. Write the letters.

A A A A A A A

O O O O O O O

JOINING ALERT

A is joined to the letter that follows, but O is not.

Write the words and sentences.

Alabama Oklahoma

America is beautiful.

Our flag flies proudly.

Better Letters

Make sure to close A and O.
Write: A not A O not O

Use your best handwriting to write the letters again.

Find a downcurve in each letter. Write the letters.

D D D D D D D

C C C C C C C

JOINING ALERT

C is joined to the letter that follows, but D is not.

Write the words and sentences.

David Deb Cam Cindy

Dan speaks Chinese.

Chinese is fun to learn.

Better Letters

Close D. Make sure C has good slant.
Write: D not D C not C

Use your best handwriting to write the letters again.

Shape

Circle your three best uppercase letters with a downcurve beginning.

Write Downcurve Letters

Find a downcurve in this letter. Write the letter.

E E E E E E E

JOINING ALERT

E is joined to the letter that follows.

Write the words and sentences.

Encino Erie Elkhart

Eddie Eve Evan Elly

Eve spied an eagle's nest.

Eaglets are baby eagles.

Better Letters

Make a loop in E. Write: E not E

Use your best handwriting to write the letter again.

Shape

Circle your three best letters with an undercurve ending.

Practice

Write the names of desert places.

El Paso, Texas

Oraibi, Arizona

Death Valley, California

Deserts are dry places. Cactus plants live there. Only a few animals do. After rain a desert blooms.

Write the paragraph about deserts. Begin each sentence with an uppercase letter.

Shape

Keys to Legibility

My writing has good shape. ☐

Write Curve Forward Letters

Find a curve forward stroke in each letter. Write the letters.

n n n n n n n

m m m m m m m

JOINING ALERT

n and m are joined to the letter that follows.

Write the words and sentences.

Nevada Maryland Maine

Nell went to Montana.

Mountain hikes were fun.

Better Letters

Start m and n just under the headline.
Write: m not m n not n

Use your best handwriting to write the letters again.

Size

Circle your three best tall letters.

Find a curve forward stroke in each letter. Write the letters.

H H

K K

JOINING ALERT

H and K are joined to the letter that follows.

Write the words and sentences.

Hawaii Kahului Kauai

Kate likes Honolulu.

Her dad saw orchids there.

Better Letters

Lift after the first stroke for H and K.
Write: H not H K not K

Use your best handwriting to write the letters again.

Write Curve Forward Letters

Find a curve forward stroke in each letter. Write the letters.

U U

Y Y

JOINING ALERT

U and Y are joined to the letter that follows.

Write the words and sentences.

Utah New York Yuma

The United States is vast.

You and I live there.

Better *Letters*

Start U and Y with a curve forward stroke.
Write: U not U Y not Y

Use your best handwriting to write the letters again.

Size

Circle your three best letters that have a descender.

Practice

Write the names of Native American peoples.

Hopi Yamasee

Kickapoo Natchez Navajo

Huron Maya Yuma Ute

Navajo art is beautiful. Museums have some of it. Young artists make rings. How lovely they are!

Write the paragraph about Navajo art. Begin each sentence with an uppercase letter.

Keys to Legibility

My writing has good shape. ☐

My writing has good size. ☐

Manuscript Maintenance

Listed below are some famous places and their locations.

Buckingham Palace, London, England
The Eiffel Tower, Paris, France
The Great Pyramid, Giza, Egypt
The Liberty Bell, Philadelphia, Pennsylvania
The Lincoln Memorial, Washington, D.C.
The Sears Tower, Chicago, Illinois

Write the name of the famous place you would see in each city. Use your best manuscript writing.

Visit Chicago, Illinois, to see

Visit Giza, Egypt, to see

Visit London, England, to see

Visit Paris, France, to see

Visit Philadelphia, Pennsylvania, to see

Visit Washington, D.C., to see

Write Curve Forward Letters

Find a curve forward stroke in each letter. Write the letters.

Z Z Z Z Z Z Z

V V V V V V V

JOINING ALERT

Z is joined to the letter that follows, but V is not.

Write the words and sentences.

Zeke Zelda Vic Vera

Violins are called fiddles.

Zithers have strings too.

Better Letters

Start Z and V with a curve forward stroke.
Write: Z not Z V not V

Use your best handwriting to write the letters again.

Spacing

Circle your three best joinings.

Write Curve Forward Letters

Find a curve forward stroke in each letter. Write the letters.

W W W W W W W

X X X X X X X

JOINING ALERT

W and X are not joined to the letter that follows.

Write the words and sentences.

Walt Wendy Xavier

What are X rays?

X rays are beams of light.

Better Letters

Start W and X with a curve forward stroke.
Write: W not W X not X

Use your best handwriting to write the letters again.

Spacing

Circle your best spacing between letters that are not joined.

Practice

Write names of inventors.

Vladimir Zworykin

George Washington Carver

Wilbur and Orville Wright

Wheels turn on axles.
X rays show bones.
Zippers fasten jackets.
My VCR records and plays.

Write the sentences about inventions. Begin each sentence with an uppercase letter.

Keys to Legibility

Shape
Size
Spacing

My writing has good shape. ☐
My writing has good size. ☐
My writing has good spacing. ☐

Write Overcurve Letters

Find an overcurve (in each letter. Write the letters.

I I I I I I I

J J J J J J J

Q Q Q Q Q Q Q

JOINING ALERT

J is joined to the letter that follows, but I and Q are not.

Write the words.

Inez Justin Quinn

Ivette Jane Quincy

Better Letters

Write: I not I, J not J, Q not Q

Use your best handwriting to write the letters again.

Slant

Circle three letters you wrote that have good slant.

Write Doublecurve Letters

Find a doublecurve / in each letter. Write the letters.

T T T T T T T

F F F F F F F

JOINING ALERT

T and F are not joined to the letter that follows.

Write the words and sentences.

Tara Tim Fran Fred

Forests keep us healthy.

Their leaves make oxygen.

Better *Letters*

Lift after the curve forward and right stroke.
Write: T not T F not F

Use your best handwriting to write the letters again.

Slant

Circle three words you wrote that have good slant.

Practice

Write the names of coastal cities.

Iwaki, Japan

Tocopilla, Chile

Qingdao, China

Tsunamis are huge waves. Floods come if one hits. I saw one once on television. Japan has tsunamis.

Write the paragraph about tsunamis. Begin each sentence with an uppercase letter.

Keys to Legibility

Shape
Size
Spacing
Slant

- My writing has good shape. ☐
- My writing has good size. ☐
- My writing has good spacing. ☐
- My writing has good slant. ☐

Write Undercurve-Loop Letters

Find an undercurve-loop ℓ in each letter. Write the letters.

G G G G G G G

S S S S S S S

L L L L L L L

JOINING ALERT

G, S, and L are not joined to the letter that follows.

Write names of places.

The Statue of Liberty

The Golden Gate Bridge

Better Letters

Remember to keep loops open.
Write: G not G, S not S, L not L

Use your best handwriting to write the letters again.

Shape

Circle your three best letters with a loop.

Write Undercurve-Slant Letters

Find an undercurve-slant / in each letter. Write the letters.

P P P P P P P

R R R R R R R

B B B B B B B

JOINING ALERT

R is joined to the letter that follows, but P and B are not.

Write the names of cities.

Phoenix Raleigh Buffalo

Boulder Philadelphia

Better Letters

Begin with an undercurve stroke.
Write: P not P, R not R, B not B

Use your best handwriting to write the letters again.

Shape

Circle your three best letters with an undercurve beginning.

Practice

Write the names of baseball teams.

Boston Red Sox

Pittsburgh Pirates

San Francisco Giants

Learn to bicycle safely. Put on a helmet. Grab handles firmly. Stop at stop signs.

Write the paragraph about bicycling. Begin each sentence with an uppercase letter.

Keys to Legibility

Shape
Size
Spacing
Slant

- My writing has good shape. ☐
- My writing has good size. ☐
- My writing has good spacing. ☐
- My writing has good slant. ☐

Uppercase Review

Write downcurve letters.

A O D C E

Write curve forward letters.

N M H K U Y Z V W X

Write overcurve letters.

I J Q

Write doublecurve letters.

T F

Write undercurve-loop letters.

G S L

Write undercurve-slant letters.

P R B

Write the names of cities.

Ithaca Toledo Seattle

Baltimore Dallas Xenia

Remember! These letters are joined to the letter that follows.

A C E H J K
M N R U Y Z

These letters are not.

B D F G I L O
P Q S T V W X

Write these song titles. Remember to use quotation marks.

"America the Beautiful"

"Yankee Doodle"

"Texas, Our Texas"

"This Land Is Your Land"

"Georgia On My Mind"

"Hawaii Ponoi"

Manuscript Maintenance

Using a Time Line

This time line is out of order. Use manuscript to write the dates and events in order below.

U.S. Flying Firsts

1929	1903	1958	1932	1927	1926
Richard E. Byrd and crew fly over South Pole	Wright Brothers make first piloted power flight	Boeing 707 is first passenger jetliner to fly U.S.–Europe	Amelia Earhart is first woman to fly solo across the Atlantic Ocean	Charles A. Lindbergh flies solo across the Atlantic Ocean	Richard E. Byrd and Floyd Bennett fly over North Pole

1903

Making a Flow Chart

A flow chart shows steps in a process. This chart shows how steel is made from iron ore. Use manuscript to write the steps in order in the flow chart. Make your writing fit the space.

Iron Into Steel

4	7	1	6	3	5	2
Oxygen is mixed into the liquid iron.	The steel is made into cars, bridges, trains, and buildings.	Iron ore is mined out of the earth.	The liquid steel cools and hardens into blocks.	At 3,000° F, the iron becomes liquid.	The iron and oxygen change into liquid steel.	The ore is put in a hot furnace.

1.

2.

3.

4.

5.

6.

7.

Writing for Yourself

Sometimes you write just for yourself. When you write for yourself, you don't have to be as neat as when you write for someone else. But your writing must still be legible. You should be able to read what you have written now and at some future time, too.

For example, you might write a journal or diary entry that is for your eyes only. In the space below, write a journal entry that tells what you did yesterday.

Date:

The more you practice writing in cursive, the easier it will be. In the following pages, you will write for yourself by making a schedule and taking notes. You will write in a new, smaller size, too. You will focus on the shape and size of your letters to help make your writing legible.

Keys to Legibility: Shape and Size

Make your writing easy to read. As you write cursive, pay attention to the shape and size of your writing.

Now that you know how to form each letter, you can write smaller and faster. Here are some things to remember.

Your tall letters should not touch the headline. Write some tall letters.

t T h H l L b B k K

Your short letters should be half the size of your tall letters. Write some short letters.

a c e i m n o r x u

Your descenders should not go too far below the baseline. Write letters with descenders.

f g j J p q y Y z Z

Remember, there are four basic strokes in cursive writing.

Undercurve *e S t G*

Write some undercurve letters.

Overcurve *n I v J*

Write some overcurve letters.

Downcurve *a E d O*

Write some downcurve letters.

Slant *l P h R*

Write some letters with slant strokes.

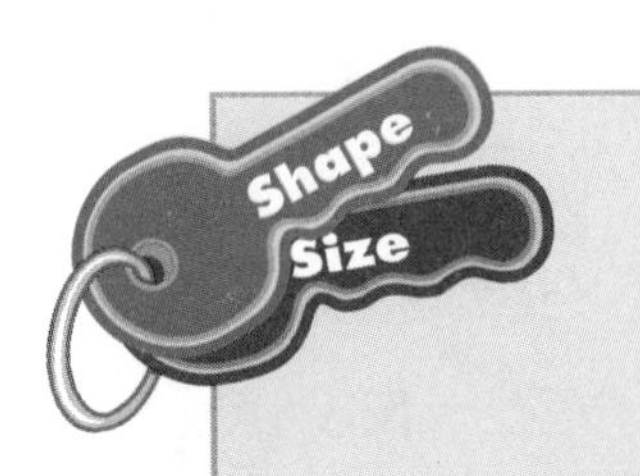

Does your writing have good shape?	Yes	No
Did you write in the new size?	Yes	No
Are all your tall letters the same size?	Yes	No
Are all your short letters the same size?	Yes	No

Make a Schedule

Writing a schedule can help you remember things you must do and places you must be. It can also help you remember the order in which you will do things. Here is a schedule:

Monday	4:00	basketball practice in gym
	5:00	help Mom wash Rover
Tuesday	3:00	Service Club meeting
Wednesday		

Add these items to the schedule:

Tuesday	8:00	surprise party for Grandma
Wednesday	7:00	social studies project with Judy, Kamal, and T'Aysha

COLLISION ALERT Make sure that your tall letters do not bump into the descenders above them.

Shape Size

Do your letters have good shape?	Yes	No
The short letters are half the size of tall letters.	Yes	No
The numerals are the size of tall letters.	Yes	No
The descenders do not go down too far.	Yes	No

On Your Own

Use cursive to write a schedule of things you might do next week.

Monday

Tuesday

Wednesday

Thursday

Friday

Saturday

Is your schedule legible?	Yes	No
Will you be able to read it next week?	Yes	No

Take Notes

When you take notes from a book, write the title and author. Then write the important facts in your own words.

Flight! by Harry Roberts
1804 — Sir George Cayley builds and flies first successful glider
1896 — Samuel P. Langley flies model of a steam-powered airplane over Potomac River
1900–1903 — Orville and Wilbur Wright build and test glider

Write the notes. Make sure your writing is legible.

Do your letters have good shape?	Yes	No
Are all your tall letters the same size?	Yes	No
Are all your short letters the same size?	Yes	No

On Your Own

Take notes from the following paragraph.
Pay attention to the size of your tall and short letters.

Flight! by Harry Roberts

On December 17, 1903, Orville and Wilbur Wright flew their plane from Kitty Hawk, North Carolina, four times. The soil was sandy and soft so they would not get badly hurt when they crashed. The first flight was 12 seconds long. The fourth flight covered 852 feet in 59 seconds. The Wright brothers had made history. They were the first people to fly a heavier-than-air machine with an engine.

Title and author:

Who flew?

Where?

When?

Why are the Wright brothers famous?

Are all your tall letters the same size? Yes No

Writing for Someone Else

Sometimes you write things for someone else to read. When you write for someone else, you must be sure that your writing is legible.

Juan took this phone message for his sister.

Thursday

Maria,
Sophia Martin called at 10:00. Your job interview at J.P. Insurance Company will be on Monday at 4:00. Good luck!
Juan

What makes Juan's message legible? Check each true statement.

- ☐ There is space for O between letters.
- ☐ There is space for \ between words.
- ☐ There is space for O between sentences.

Add this message to the pad.

P.S. Call 555-1235 if you can't make it. She'll be in the office until 5:00.

In the following pages, you will write an invitation, a thank-you note, a friendly letter, a recipe, and a school paper. As you write, you will focus on spacing to help make your writing legible.

Keys to Legibility: Spacing

You are writing smaller with good shape and size. Now look at your spacing between letters, words, and sentences. Your writing will be easy to read if the spacing is correct.

Between Letters There should be enough space for *o*.

handwriting

Between Words There should be enough space for \ .

This\word\spacing\is\correct.

Between Sentences There should be enough space for O .

Good spacing makes writing legible. O Shape and size do, too.

Write the note below. Use good spacing between letters and words.

Mary,
Please remember that it is your turn to walk Skippy.
Bye! Chris

Spacing

Is there space for *o* between letters?	Yes	No
Is there space for \ between words?	Yes	No

Write an Invitation

Use your best handwriting when you write an invitation. Use the information below to fill out the party invitation.

- *the party is for Andrea*
- *the date is May 25*
- *the time is 1:00*
- *the address is 62 Sunset Avenue*
  Ogden, Utah
- *RSVP by May 15 to 555-7716*

Is your writing legible?	Yes	No
Is there space for *O* between letters?	Yes	No
Is there space for \ between words?	Yes	No

Write a Thank-You Note

Here is a thank-you note that Andrea wrote after her party.

June 5

Dear Matt,

Thank you for helping me decorate the yard for my party. There was so much to do! The yard looked great. Thank you again.

Your friend,

Andrea

Write Andrea's thank-you note to Matt or write a note to thank someone who has helped you.

Spacing

Is your writing legible?	Yes	No
Is there space for O between sentences?	Yes	No

Write a Friendly Letter

Read this friendly letter. Notice its five parts.

581 Ashley Court
Hickory, North Carolina 28601 ← heading
March 5, _____

Dear Brittany, ← greeting

Great news! I got a puppy! I named her Button because she is small and round. She has fluffy brown fur and cute little ears. ← body
I heard you made the track team. Good work!

Your friend, ← closing
Nico ← signature

Write the body of a letter to a friend. Pay attention to the spacing between letters, words, and sentences.

Spacing

Is your writing legible? Yes No

Write a Recipe

When you write a recipe, list the steps in order.

A Fishy Dish

1. Mix one can of tuna and four tablespoons of mayonnaise in a bowl.
2. Spoon the tuna onto a plate and make it into the shape of a fish.
3. Put lettuce leaves on for fins and a tail.
4. Use an olive for the eye.
5. Use a strip of green pepper to make a mouth.
6. Put 12 cherry tomato "bubbles" around the fish.

Write the steps from the recipe above.

Is there space for \ between words? Yes No

Write for School

When you write for school, you usually write a heading and a title on your paper. The heading might contain your name, your teacher's name, the subject, and the date.

Write the paragraph to complete Taylor's paper.

Our class should visit the aquarium. We can get there by bus. We could see the giant saltwater tank. We might see the sharks being fed.

Taylor Sheets
Mrs. Johnson
Science
April 17

My Idea for a Class Trip

Ask a friend to read and evaluate your writing.

Is the writing legible? Yes No

On Your Own

Complete the heading on this paper. Then write a paragraph about a trip that your class should take. Give at least three reasons why the class should take this trip.

Name:
Teacher:
Subject:
Date:

Title:

Spacing

Is there space for O between letters?	Yes	No
Is there space for \ between words?	Yes	No
Is there space for O between sentences?	Yes	No

Writing for Publication

When you write things that many people will read, you are writing for publication. Your writing must be legible. You should use your best handwriting for your final draft.

On the following pages, you will use the writing process to write a news story for a class newspaper. You will plan, draft, revise, edit, and write your final draft. Then you will publish your news story. As you write, you will focus on slant to help make your writing legible.

To begin, write a list of ideas for your class newspaper. Work together with your classmates. Jot down your ideas for names for your newspaper, what kinds of articles will be in it, and what kinds of illustrations it may have.

Names for Paper	**Articles**	**Illustrations**

Keys to Legibility: Uniform Slant

You are writing smaller and are using good shape, size, and spacing. Now you can concentrate on uniform slant. Your writing will be easier to read if all your letters slant the same way.

Using good paper position will help you write with uniform slant.

If you are left-handed . . .

If you are right-handed . . .

POSITION • Check your paper position.

PULL • Pull your downstrokes in the proper direction.

SHIFT • Shift your paper as you write.

Write the sentence. Use uniform slant.

Writing with uniform slant makes my writing easy to read.

Check your slant.

Draw lines through the slant strokes of the letters.

Your slant should look like

uniform, not *uniform*.

Write a News Story

A news story is a factual report about a current event. It uses facts to tell about the event. A news story does not tell the writer's opinion.

Follow these steps for writing a news story.

I. Prewriting
Start by thinking about a topic for your news story. Imagine that your readers will be the students in your class. **Brainstorm** topics to add to the list below. Write legibly so you can read your ideas later.

OAK HILL SCHOOL NEWS

WE WON!

Soccer team wins final game

Dog Saves Baby Kitten

school team wins a big game
class visitors
new student in class
school concert
new class pet
school play opens

Look back at your list. Choose your topic. Write the subject of your news story below.

Answer the "5W's and H" questions to plan your news story.

What happened?

Who was involved?

When did it happen?

Where did it happen?

Why did it happen?

How did it happen?

News stories start with the most important facts and end with the least important. List facts for your news story from most important to least important.

Most important

Least important

2. Drafting

Write your first draft. Begin your news story with a sentence that will get your readers' attention.

Slant

Is your writing legible?	Yes	No
Did you position your paper correctly?	Yes	No
Does your writing have uniform slant?	Yes	No

3. Revising

Read your draft and mark any changes you want to make. You may want to ask a classmate to help you. Use the editing marks below as you revise your news story.

≡	Make a capital.	∧	Insert or add.
/	Use lowercase.	℘	Delete or take out.
⊙	Add a period.	¶	Indent for a new paragraph.

4. Editing

Check your news story for errors in spelling, punctuation, and capitalization. Then answer the questions below to help you check your handwriting. You may want to ask a classmate to help you.

Do your letters have good shape?	Yes	No
Are all your tall letters the same size?	Yes	No
Are your short letters half the size of your tall letters?	Yes	No
Did you avoid collisions?	Yes	No
Is there space for O between letters?	Yes	No
Is there space for \ between words?	Yes	No
Is there space for O between sentences?	Yes	No
Does your writing have uniform slant?	Yes	No
Is your writing legible?	Yes	No

5. Publishing

Use your best handwriting to make a final copy of your news story. Then follow these steps to publish your news story:

- Add a title.
- Add your name as a byline.
- Add an illustration, if you wish.
- Post your story on a bulletin board with everyone else's story.
- Read the class newspaper!

Writing Quickly

Writing quickly is a skill that you need to draft a story, write a timed test, or take notes as your teacher talks. Writing that is done quickly should still be easy to read. With practice, you will learn how to make your writing speedy and legible.

Read the lines of poetry below. They are part of a poem written by Julia A. Fletcher Carney in 1845. Write the poem quickly and legibly.

Little drops of water,
Little grains of sand,
Make the mighty ocean
And the pleasant land.

Little drops of water,
Little grains of sand,
Make the mighty ocean
And the pleasant land.

Write the lines of poetry again. Try to write faster, but make sure your writing is legible.

Little drops of water,
Little grains of sand,
Make the mighty ocean
and the pleasant land.

Write the lines of poetry two more times. Try to write even faster, but keep your writing easy to read.

Little drops of water.
Little grains of sand,
make the mighty ocean and
the pleasant land.

Little drop of water.
Little grains of sand,
make the night ocean and the
pleasant land.

Now read your final writing. Circle Yes or No to respond to each statement. Then show your writing to someone, either a classmate or your teacher. Ask that person to circle Yes or No beside each statement.

	My Evaluation	My Classmate's or Teacher's Evaluation
The writing is easy to read.	Yes No	Yes No
The writing has good Shape .	Yes No	Yes No
The writing has good Size .	Yes No	Yes No
The writing has good Spacing .	Yes No	Yes No
The writing has good Slant .	Yes No	Yes No

Writing Easily

As you write stories and essays for school papers and tests, it is important that your handwriting flows easily. When you automatically know how to write legibly, you don't have to worry about your handwriting. You are free to think about what you want your writing to say. With practice, you will learn how to make your writing easy, quick, and legible.

Read the writing prompt below. Respond to it by writing on the lines. Let your handwriting flow easily as you think and write.

Descriptive Writing

Think about a place you have visited.

Write a description of the place you have visited. Include details to help the reader see the place you are describing.

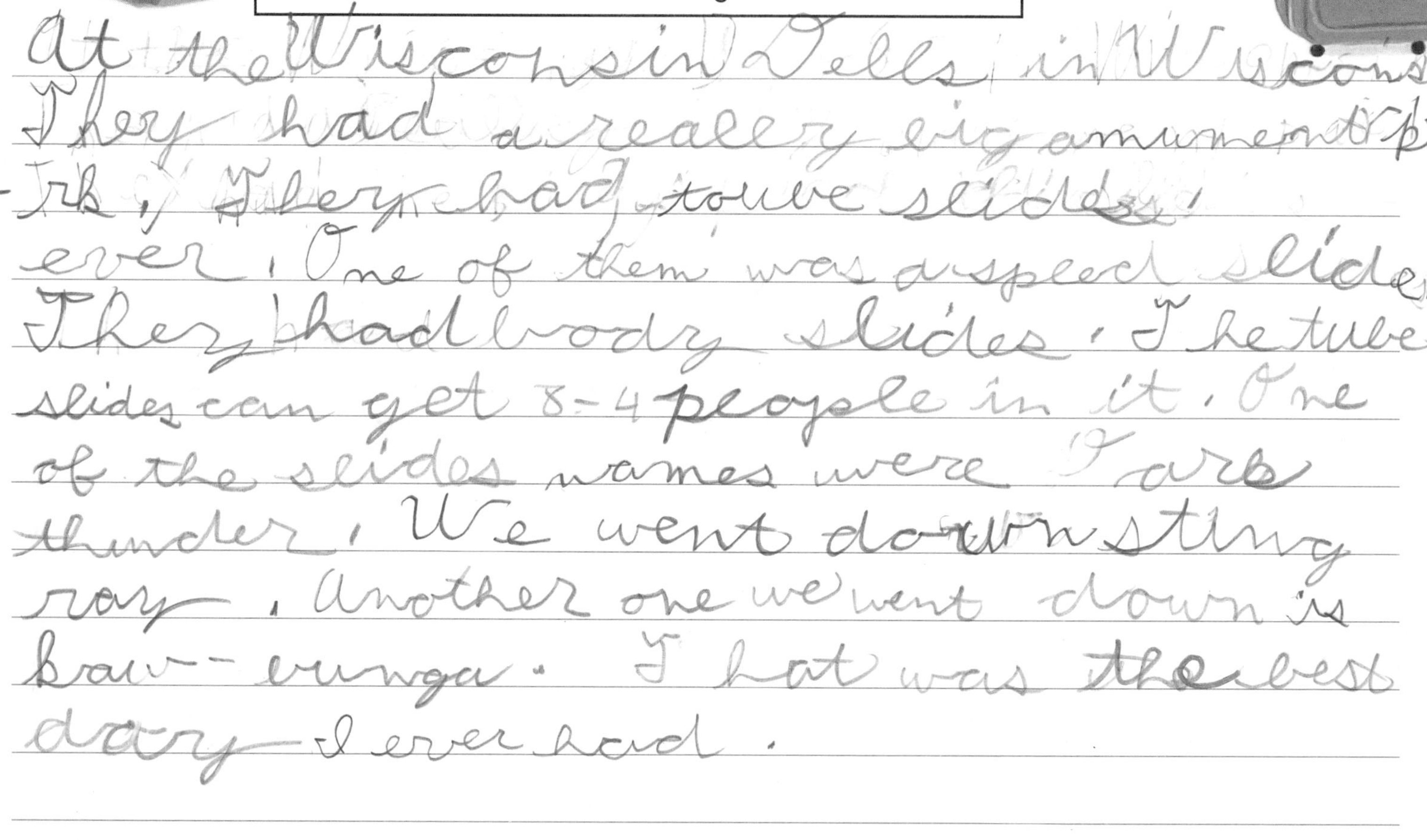

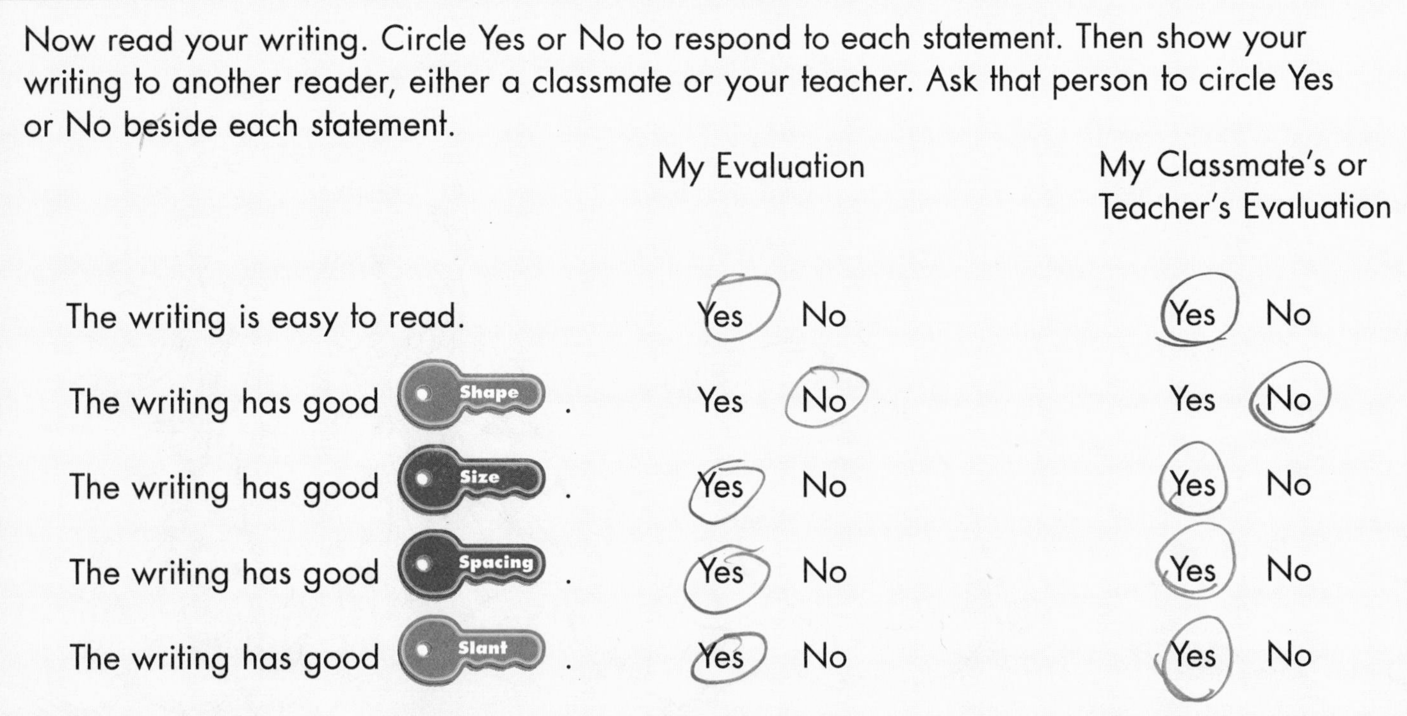

Now read your writing. Circle Yes or No to respond to each statement. Then show your writing to another reader, either a classmate or your teacher. Ask that person to circle Yes or No beside each statement.

	My Evaluation	My Classmate's or Teacher's Evaluation
The writing is easy to read.	Yes No	Yes No
The writing has good Shape.	Yes No	Yes No
The writing has good Size.	Yes No	Yes No
The writing has good Spacing.	Yes No	Yes No
The writing has good Slant.	Yes No	Yes No

Posttest

It's Dark in Here

I am writing these poems
From inside a lion,
And it's rather dark in here.
So please excuse the handwriting
Which may not be too clear.
But this afternoon by the lion's cage
I'm afraid I got too near.
And I'm writing these lines
From inside a lion,
And it's rather dark in here.

by Shel Silverstein

Write the poem in your best cursive handwriting.

~~Its Dark in here.~~

I am writing these poems
from inside a lion,
And it's rather dark in here.
So please excuse the handwriting
Which may not be too clear.
But this afternoon by the lion's cage
I'm afraid I got too near.
And I'm writing these lines
From inside a lion,
And it's rather dark in here.

by Shel Silverstein

Is your writing easy to read? Yes No

Write your five best cursive letters.

a C E G I

Write five cursive letters you would like to improve.

B D F H g

Handwriting and the Writing Process

Write a Paragraph

A paragraph is a group of sentences about one subject. Use the steps below to write a paragraph about how to play your favorite game.

1. **Prewriting**
   Prewriting means gathering ideas and planning before you write. List your ideas on a piece of paper. Then plan your paragraph, telling the subject and in what order you will write your ideas.

2. **Drafting**
   Drafting means putting your thoughts into written sentences for the first time. Use the ideas you listed in Prewriting to draft your paragraph. Write your first draft.

3. **Revising**
   Revising means changing your writing to make it say exactly what you mean. Read your draft. Mark any changes you want to make.

   Does your writing include all the information readers want to know? Yes No

   Does your writing include descriptive details? Yes No

4. **Editing**
   Editing means checking your revised writing for errors in spelling, punctuation, capitalization, and handwriting.

   Are all words spelled correctly? Yes No

   Have you used uppercase letters and punctuation correctly? Yes No

   Do your letters have good shape and size? Yes No

   Is there good spacing between letters, words, and sentences? Yes No

   Does your writing have uniform slant? Yes No

   Is your writing easy to read? Yes No

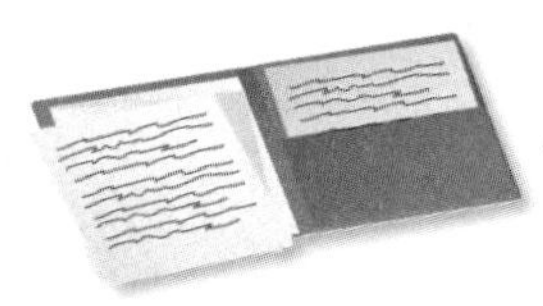

5. **Publishing**
   Publishing means using your best handwriting to make an error-free copy of your writing. Share your writing.

Record of Student's Handwriting Skills

Cursive

	Needs Improvement	Shows Mastery
Sits correctly	☐	☐
Holds pencil correctly	☐	☐
Positions paper correctly	☐	☐
Writes numerals **1-10**	☐	☐
Writes undercurve letters: **i, t, u, w, e, l**	☐	☐
Writes undercurve letters: **b, h, f, k, r, s, j, p**	☐	☐
Writes downcurve letters: **a, d, g, o, c, q**	☐	☐
Writes overcurve letters: **n, m, y, x, v, z**	☐	☐
Writes downcurve letters: **A, O, D, C, E**	☐	☐
Writes curve forward letters: **N, M, H, K, U, Y**	☐	☐
Writes curve forward letters: **Z, V, W, X**	☐	☐
Writes overcurve letters: **I, J, Q**	☐	☐
Writes doublecurve letters: **T, F**	☐	☐
Writes undercurve-loop letters: **G, S, L**	☐	☐
Writes undercurve-slant letters: **P, R, B**	☐	☐
Writes the undercurve to undercurve joining	☐	☐

	Needs Improvement	Shows Mastery
Writes the undercurve to downcurve joining	☐	☐
Writes the undercurve to overcurve joining	☐	☐
Writes the overcurve to undercurve joining	☐	☐
Writes the overcurve to downcurve joining	☐	☐
Writes the overcurve to overcurve joining	☐	☐
Writes the checkstroke to undercurve joining	☐	☐
Writes the checkstroke to downcurve joining	☐	☐
Writes the checkstroke to overcurve joining	☐	☐
Writes in the new size	☐	☐
Writes with correct shape	☐	☐
Writes with correct size	☐	☐
Writes with correct spacing	☐	☐
Writes with uniform slant	☐	☐
Writes legibly for self	☐	☐
Writes legibly for someone else	☐	☐
Writes legibly for publication	☐	☐
Regularly checks written work for legibility	☐	☐

Index